Shtick

by Henry Meyerson

A Samuel French Acting Edition

SAMUEL FRENCH
FOUNDED 1830
NEW YORK HOLLYWOOD LONDON TORONTO

SAMUELFRENCH.COM

Copyright © 2009 by Henry Meyerson

ALL RIGHTS RESERVED

CAUTION: Professionals and amateurs are hereby warned that *SHTICK* is subject to a royalty. It is fully protected under the copyright laws of the United States of America, the British Commonwealth, including Canada, and all other countries of the Copyright Union. All rights, including professional, amateur, motion picture, recitation, lecturing, public reading, radio broadcasting, television and the rights of translation into foreign languages are strictly reserved. In its present form the play is dedicated to the reading public only.

The amateur live stage performance rights to *SHTICK* are controlled exclusively by Samuel French, Inc., and royalty arrangements and licenses must be secured well in advance of presentation. PLEASE NOTE that amateur royalty fees are set upon application in accordance with your producing circumstances. When applying for a royalty quotation and license please give us the number of performances intended, dates of production, your seating capacity and admission fee. Royalties are payable one week before the opening performance of the play to Samuel French, Inc., at 45 W. 25th Street, New York, NY 10010.

Royalty of the required amount must be paid whether the play is presented for charity or gain and whether or not admission is charged.

Stock royalty quoted upon application to Samuel French, Inc.

For all other rights than those stipulated above, apply to Samuel French, Inc., at 45 W. 25th Street, New York, NY 10010.

Particular emphasis is laid on the question of amateur or professional readings, permission and terms for which must be secured in writing from Samuel French, Inc.

Copying from this book in whole or in part is strictly forbidden by law, and the right of performance is not transferable.

Whenever the play is produced the following notice must appear on all programs, printing and advertising for the play: "Produced by special arrangement with Samuel French, Inc."

Due authorship credit must be given on all programs, printing and advertising for the play.

No one shall commit or authorize any act or omission by which the copyright of, or the right to copyright, this play may be impaired.

No one shall make any changes in this play for the purpose of production.

Publication of this play does not imply availability for performance. Both amateurs and professionals considering a production are strongly advised in their own interests to apply to Samuel French, Inc., for written permission before starting rehearsals, advertising, or booking a theatre.

No part of this book may be reproduced, stored in a retrieval system, or transmitted in any form, by any means, now known or yet to be invented, including mechanical, electronic, photocopying, recording, videotaping, or otherwise, without the prior written permission of the publisher.

IMPORTANT BILLING AND CREDIT REQUIREMENTS

All producers of *SHTICK must* give credit to the Author of the Play in all programs distributed in connection with performances of the Play, and in all instances in which the title of the Play appears for the purposes of advertising, publicizing or otherwise exploiting the Play and/or a production. The name of the Author *must* appear on a separate line on which no other name appears, immediately following the title and *must* appear in size of type not less than fifty percent of the size of the title type.

CAST

- **HELEN** (60) - A woman who is ready and able to cope not only with her husband Murray's physical problems, but his rotten disposition, as well. She radiates energy and is as skilled at verbal repartee as Murray.
- **MURRAY** (60) - Murray is in a wheel chair and partially paralyzed. Having always been sarcastic and irascible, his stroke certainly hasn't improved his disposition.
- **GLADYS** (55) - Helen's freewheeling, younger sister. More stylishly attired than Helen, but perhaps a tad too glitzy. While she is no match for Helen's verbal ability, she is the breezier, more self-assured of the sisters. Gladys lives by the creed of honesty and having a good time.

PLACE

Helen and Murray's living room

TIME

Present

Among the many mysteries of life two stand out in my mind: 1) Why are some people able to stay married for endlessly blissful years, and 2) What makes people laugh? While writing SHTICK, I discovered that often these two mysteries are intertwined. Which leads me to Ronnie, my wife of endlessly blissful and laugh filled years.

- Henry Meyerson

ACT ONE

(SETTING: A hospital waiting area.)

(AT LIGHTS: **HELEN** *is pacing.* **GLADYS** *enters.)*

HELEN. Thanks for coming, Gladys. Hospitals are not really people friendly places.

GLADYS. Not a problem. We're sisters, right? Where else should I be? So, tell me what happened.

HELEN. He was in the middle of one of his jigs…

GLADYS. He was dancing?

HELEN. I meant gigs. I always get that wrong. Gigs.

GLADYS. Where?

HELEN. What difference does it make?

GLADYS. No difference. Go ahead.

HELEN. I will if you promise not to ask a bunch of your silly questions.

GLADYS. Go ahead.

HELEN. He was in the middle of one of his…performances…in New Jersey, okay?

GLADYS. Figures. Okay.

HELEN. Why does it figure?

GLADYS. He loved New Jersey.

HELEN. How do you know?

GLADYS. It's not important. Go ahead.

HELEN. So Jack said…

GLADYS. His agent?

HELEN. Yes, his agent. How do you know his agent?

GLADYS. Never mind. Go ahead.

HELEN. Jack, said…he said…

*(***HELEN*** begins to cry.)*

GLADYS. That's okay, Helen.

HELEN. I'm not asking permission, Gladys.

GLADYS. So Jack said…

HELEN. Jack said Murray just collapsed. Just fell over. The microphone fell on top of him. He fell and didn't move.

GLADYS. Then?

HELEN. Then? He just laid there, Gladys. The audience thought it was part of the act. He laid there with the God damn microphone on top of him and the audience laughed their asses off. Finally, Jack got some guys to carry him off and he wound up here.

GLADYS. How awful.

HELEN. I got the call last night. They rushed him here.

GLADYS. This is a great place, Helen. He'll get great care.

HELEN. How do you know?

GLADYS. I dated some doctors from here.

HELEN. You dated doctors from everywhere.

GLADYS. Let's not discuss my sex life now.

HELEN. You're right. I'm sorry.

GLADYS. You've always been critical of my dating.

HELEN. Only because you haven't been.

GLADYS. Haven't been dating?

HELEN. Haven't been critical.

GLADYS. I'm here for you, Helen. Get off me.

HELEN. "Get off you" is a line Murray would never pass up, but I'll let it go.

GLADYS. How come Brenda isn't here?

HELEN. She was here last night and this morning. It's not easy for her to see her father like this. If the coma doesn't end soon, she might not have to come back.

GLADYS. Morbid thinking, Helen. Stop that.

HELEN. I'm just telling you what the doctor said.

GLADYS. It's that serious?

HELEN. The stroke was big and he thinks it made a lot of damage. They won't really know how much until he wakes up. If he wakes up. Until then, we wait.

GLADYS. He's such a young man.

HELEN. Not if you saw him now.

GLADYS. In his prime.

HELEN. Let's not push it, Gladys. Sixty years might be good for wine, but not necessarily for a stand-up comic. I hate seeing him like this. With all the tubes and pipes going in and out of him he looks like a bag-pipe.

GLADYS. Given the situation, the news about Murray, I have to tell you something, Helen.

HELEN. I know.

GLADYS. You do?

HELEN. And I thank you for it.

GLADYS. Really? Why?

HELEN. Why? Because you're a nice person, that's why. And because you're my little sister, that's why.

GLADYS. But I'm not a nice person, Helen. That's part of what I want to tell you.

HELEN. Why would you want to tell me that?

GLADYS. To set the record straight.

HELEN. Gladys, you don't have to explain why you came here to be with me. That's what family does.

GLADYS. That's not what this is all about.

HELEN. What then?

GLADYS. I just hope this doesn't cause tension between us.

HELEN. No more than I'm feeling by this conversation at this moment.

GLADYS. Good. Because not only are we sisters, but good friends and you have to believe I treasure our relationship.

HELEN. This is starting to worry me, Gladys. Tell me now. What the hell are you getting at?

GLADYS. *(said quickly, to the point of being unintelligible)* I had an affair with Murray.

HELEN. What? I didn't...

GLADYS. *(said as above)* I had an affair with Murray.

HELEN. If you don't slow down, I'm going to hit you.

GLADYS. *(normal)* I had an affair with Murray.

HELEN. What?

GLADYS. I had an affair…

HELEN. STOP! I heard you. I just don't understand you.

GLADYS. It started three years ago. I thought it would be important for you to know, in case, you know… Murray…well…

HELEN. I still don't…

GLADYS. We bumped into each other at the Jersey shore. He was appearing at…

HELEN. …yeah, I know what he does, Gladys.

GLADYS. We talked, had a few drinks…

HELEN. …I said, I know what he does, Gladys. What I want to know is why.

GLADYS. Maybe it was the alcohol.

HELEN. For three years? What the hell were you two drinking?

GLADYS. No, I meant…

HELEN. What the hell were you two thinking?

GLADYS. I'm not sure what…

HELEN. HOW COULD YOU DO THIS TO ME?

GLADYS. Stop yelling at me. This is very difficult for me, too.

HELEN. Not like for me, Gladys. And why would you tell me? Did I really need to know this? Did I really need to know this now?

GLADYS. I've always believed that before a person dies, everything should be laid out on the table.

HELEN. Just like you were laid out in bed.

GLADYS. That's uncalled for, Helen.

HELEN. You figured when you told me, I was going to kill you, and you wanted to make sure you died with a confession on your lips.

GLADYS. I was talking about Murray, not me. You're misinterpreting what I said.

HELEN. The only thing I misinterpreted was just how stupid our parents' kids were. Particularly me. Murray, the only snake with a visible dick and Gladys the only sister with no visible conscience. How stupid am I? How did I miss this?

GLADYS. Oh, I don't think you're stupid, Helen. You were always the brighter of us.

HELEN. I used to think so.

GLADYS. You always got better grades.

HELEN. THIS ISN'T ABOUT GRADES. THIS IS ABOUT TRUST. *(beat)* I'm getting dizzy.

GLADYS. I'll get a chair.

HELEN. Don't bother. When I sit down you'll probably pull it out from under me.

GLADYS. I would never…

HELEN. Bullshit. You already did.

GLADYS. I think you're taking this a little…

HELEN. You knew about Jersey. You knew about Jack. YOU KNOW WHERE HIS GOD DAMN BIRTHMARK IS.

GLADYS. Calm down, Helen. You don't want to have a…

HELEN. Stroke? Why not? I can move into the bed next to Murray and you can visit both of us. Banging doctors for a hobby I can understand, but brother-in-laws? Your brother-in-law?

GLADYS. You always get crude when you get angry.

HELEN. You and Murray. At the beach. I'm in the Bronx under a tree with birds shitting on my head and you and Murray are romping at the shore. Beautiful.

GLADYS. No need to be sarcastic.

HELEN. That's the least I want to be. Try murderous.

GLADYS. Don't be silly. I'm your sister.

HELEN. I'm taking away your sister licence. It's revoked. Go away, Gladys.

GLADYS. You're upset, Helen, and I think someone close should stay with you at this time.

HELEN. You stayed close with Murray and look what happened.

GLADYS. I meant I should stay...

HELEN. Go home, Gladys. I'll call you if Murray gets horny.

(GLADYS starts to go, then hesitates.)

What are you stopping for. GO!

(HELEN charges off stage after GLADYS. Lights dim, then relight full on a middle class living room. A sofa stretches across the stage, in front of which is a small table. Stage rear are two doors, one to the outside, one to the kitchen.)

(HELEN enters pushing MURRAY, weary and bedraggled, in a wheel-chair. They wear jackets, MURRAY a hat and scarf. MURRAY sits forlornly, immobile, quietly watching HELEN as she bustles around making room for the wheelchair, pushing chairs around, arranging things,)

HELEN *(cont.)* Fall is on the way. You can feel the chill in the air. Always liked fall, except for the chill. Maybe someone will invent a warm fall, but that would be like spring, wouldn't it? *(laughs)*

(MURRAY stares ahead, not responding.)

That was a joke, Murray. I think you've lost your sense of humor.

(MURRAY looks away and grimaces. Undaunted, HELEN busies herself removing her coat.)

Terrible about that dog. You'd think that stupid woman would know to keep the dog on a short leash.

(HELEN touches the cuff of his pant leg.)

HELEN *(cont.)* It's dry now. I'll wash them tonight.

(She starts removing MURRAY's coat and hat. He doesn't move to help and she has a difficult time of it.)

Wish you could do this on your own. Maybe if you lost a few pounds this would be easier. Dr. Shapiro wants you to go on a diet.

(MURRAY grimaces again. In fact, he seems to be purposefully hindering her. There is a petulance about his behavior.)

Yes, I know about you and Dr. Shapiro. It wasn't his fault you fell out of the chair. You shouldn't have been chasing that guy down the hall just because he said you shuffled the cards lousy.

(**MURRAY** *begins to object, but is brushed aside by* **HELEN**'s *behavior.*)

He wasn't wrong, was he? Even before the stroke you were all thumbs so I don't understand your getting so crazy. And Shapiro is right. You better lose some weight. I can't keep moving this lard around. Shapiro told me you're the only guy in history to ever put on twenty pounds in a hospital. I'll leave your scarf on in case you get a chill.

(**MURRAY** *is mute as* **HELEN** *continues to help him with his clothing then moves to the kitchen door. She stops halfway.*)

Oh. when would you like to do your physical therapy?

(**MURRAY** *dismisses her with a wave of his right hand.*)

(*She makes the sound of a buzzer, ala a game show.*) Wrong answer. Let me rephrase the question. When would you like to do your physical therapy?

(**MURRAY** *looks away.*)

After dinner?

(**MURRAY** *doesn't reply.*)

Ah, good. So after dinner it is. Now, would you like some coffee?

(*With his right arm,* **MURRAY** *lifts his left arm and shakes it.*)

HELEN (*cont.*) What does that mean? "Yes" for coffee, or "no" for coffee? I'm still having trouble learning your signals.

(**MURRAY** *again uses his right arm to shake his useless left arm.*)

What is it with the pantomime bit?

(**MURRAY** *again uses his right arm to shake his useless left arm.*)

The hospital bracelet?

(**MURRAY** *nods.* **HELEN** *gets a scissors from the table and cuts off the bracelet.*)

I don't know why they put a name tag on you every time you go for rehab. I know who you are and you're sure not going to wander off. *(beat)* Now, would you like some coffee?

(**MURRAY** *slowly nods his head as* **HELEN** *exits to the kitchen. She now speaks from off-stage.*)

I'll fix us both some coffee. *(beat)* Something to eat? *(pause)* Murray?

(**HELEN** *appears in the doorway.*)

I said, do you want something to eat?

(**MURRAY** *shakes his head no,* **HELEN** *goes back to the kitchen.*)

Well, I'm hungry so I'm eating. And the pantomime is growing thin, Murray.

(*With* **HELEN** *gone,* **MURRAY** *sits and stares morosely out at the audience. We hear* **HELEN** *bustling around the kitchen, plates banging, other noises. Finally,* **HELEN** *re-emerges carrying a tray with two cups.*)

Brenda called last night. She wants to come over today to see you.

(**MURRAY** *shakes his head "no."*)

HELEN *(cont.)* Right. That's what I figured so I told her it was your rehab day, to hold off 'till I called her. Brenda seemed really upset. Kept worrying about your "psychological adjustment." She wants you to see a shrink. She thinks you're depressed. Here, I'll hold the cup.

(**HELEN** *lifts the cup to* **MURRAY**'*s mouth and he drinks.*)

MURRAY. What makes her think I'm depressed?

HELEN. Just a wild guess.

(**HELEN** *feeds him more coffee.*)

I am too.

MURRAY. What?

HELEN. Depressed.

  (**HELEN** *feeds him more coffee.*)

  I spoke to Dr. Shapiro about it. Interesting. He says the reason I can't sleep is because I'm depressed and the reason I'm depressed is because I'm angry.

MURRAY. I have noticed you've been a little testy lately. What have you got to be angry about?

HELEN. I can't imagine. Shapiro says I should talk to you about my anger.

MURRAY. So talk.

  (**MURRAY** *nods his head as if falling asleep.*)

HELEN. That's what I told him you would do. And I told Brenda you'd sooner eat a pile of thumb tacks than talk to someone. She said she could arrange it either way.

  (**MURRAY** *smiles.*)

  I figured you would like that. I think I'll get something to eat. Want anything?

  (**MURRAY** *shakes his head "no," and* **HELEN** *exits to the kitchen.* **MURRAY** *attempts to lift the coffee cup with his right hand, but his hand wobbles spilling some coffee so he puts the cup down.* **HELEN** *enters with a piece of cake on a dish. She eats and finishes the cake as she talks.*)

HELEN *(cont.)* Listen, Murray, when are you going to quit with this "I'm paralyzed" routine? It's getting old. Let's get some new material.

  (**MURRAY** *smiles at this as* **HELEN** *lifts the cup for him to drink.*)

  You liked that one, huh? That's what comes of living with a comic. You begin to see the world as just bits of shtick. Okay, Murray, today we're going to do the one where the girl with the big tits walks by and you leer at her, jump out of the chair and follow her and this time I won't be jealous. I might even applaud. I might even get it out of your pants for you.

MURRAY. *(mumbles)* Groucho.

*(**HELEN** bends to him to hear better.)*

HELEN. What? Damn it, speak up, Murray, I can't understand.

MURRAY. Groucho.

HELEN. Yeah, I know that was Groucho's bit, but that never stopped you from using it. Murray the Shtick Thief. You liked it, you took it. You were so cocky and had that swagger. When we first met I thought you had the greatest swagger and the greatest ass. Man, the way you moved.

MURRAY. I still have a great ass.

HELEN. You're right. That's because there's so much more of it. Yep, you had a great swagger.

MURRAY. I seem to have lost that bounce in my step.

HELEN. Well, you'll get it back.

*(**MURRAY** checks the watch on his good hand.)*

MURRAY. What time should I expect it?

HELEN. That's what you have to work on, Murray. Rehab?

*(**MURRAY** leans back, dejected.)*

It would be a relief for Brenda to see that you're making progress in rehab, but you want to keep all the good stuff for yourself. Selfish, like always.

*(**MURRAY** looks away in apparent rejection of the idea.)*

HELEN *(cont.)* Wouldn't you like to relieve her mind?

*(**MURRAY** looks more beat than before, if that's possible.)*

All right. I'll drop it.

*(**MURRAY** brightens up as if nothing happened.)*

You got me again, didn't you. You are such a manipulator.

*(**MURRAY** smiles.)*

You may have had a stroke, but you haven't changed. Such smugness!

(He smiles more.)

Such arrogance!

(His smile broadens.)

Such selfishness.

MURRAY. It's a new me.

HELEN. Baloney.

*(**MURRAY** shrugs.)*

You know, this mute routine is really starting to get annoying, Murray. I couldn't tell if that shrug meant you agreed with "baloney," barely agreed, or that you didn't give a damn what I said and were falling asleep on me.

MURRAY. My shrugging has nothing to do with you.

HELEN. You silly man, of course it does. That's like saying your stroke has nothing to do with me.

MURRAY. IT DOESN'T.

HELEN. Ah, I finally got you. Would you repeat that please?

MURRAY. It doesn't have anything to do with you.

HELEN. Not at all?

MURRAY. Not like it has to do with me.

HELEN. Just like you, you selfish oaf. You always hogged everything. The bed, the TV remote, now your stroke. Self-centered for as long as I've known you.

MURRAY. In all our years together I never had anything to call my own. And now you want to jump into this stroke I had. Sorry, Helen. This stroke is all mine, so bug off.

HELEN. Nothing to call your own? How about your career, piddling as it was? And how about the freedom it gave you. Frankly, I think you had too much freedom.

MURRAY. What does that mean? Is this what Shapiro told you to say to me? Did he tell you to get me pissed off, because now I am. Damn doctors should butt out.

HELEN. Want more coffee?

MURRAY. Answer me. What does that mean, "I had too much freedom?"

HELEN. Some people can't handle freedom. They get into trouble. And I don't want to talk about it now.

MURRAY. Why not?

HELEN. It'll get us into a fight and I don't want to upset you. I don't want to be responsible for your next stroke.

MURRAY. I'll absolve you now, not to worry. And according to Shapiro, I didn't have a damn stroke. He keeps calling it a CVA. So that's what I have. I mean, he should know, right, a doctor like that. So that's it. It's only a CVA. Just a little old garden variety Cerebral Vascular Accident. Get that? An accident caused by a blood clot. Did anyone get the licence number of the blood clot that hit me?

HELEN. Don't get worked up.

MURRAY. Then tell me what you meant before about having too much freedom and "getting into trouble."

HELEN. Stop trying to harass me and bait me.

MURRAY. Well, I didn't have too much freedom and I didn't get into any trouble. Well, maybe a little trouble, but this stroke isn't because of anything I did wrong, is it?

HELEN. Want to watch some TV?

MURRAY. You didn't answer me again. Do you think this is because of something I did wrong?

HELEN. I don't know. Have you done something wrong?

MURRAY. Not a thing. *(pause)* Yeah, maybe a little TV would be a good idea.

HELEN. Too late. Now I don't want to.

MURRAY. You trying to torture me?

HELEN. As if I could. You're beyond torture, Murray. All comics are beyond torture or you wouldn't be comics.

MURRAY. Then I'd like to hear a good bedtime story. Tell me about mean little Murray and his supposed freedom.

HELEN. Were you home every night like other fathers and husbands or did you travel all over the country to do your jigs?

MURRAY. Gigs, for crying out loud. In all this time, you should once get it right. And I had no choice. I went to them because they wouldn't come to me.

HELEN. Exactly. You went to them. And because you went to them, entertained them, made them laugh, did they love you like your wife and kid loved you?

MURRAY. Of course not.

HELEN. But you went.

MURRAY. We developed the habit of eating. I made money, we ate. No money, starve. Simple concept. Besides, you knew all of this when you met me. Comic, travel. Comic, travel. In order to sell me, I had to travel.

HELEN. So then the only reason you travelled was to sell yourself, to make money. Nothing else.

MURRAY. This is the discussion you want to have now? You think this is the appropriate time to push the "Murray, you should have done it better" routine." My life was tough, Helen. You know that. You think I liked *schlepping* around the country, living out of suitcases, eating airport food, missing my kid, missing you.

HELEN. I don't know. You tell me. How did you feel about it?

MURRAY. When I was clicking it was an unbelievable high. That's it. Being a comic made me feel high.

HELEN. High enough for you to not be with me.

MURRAY. I gotta be honest. Sometimes it was a close call.

HELEN. I've noticed through the years, when you get honest, I get hurt. When you say, "I gotta be honest," I wonder what you are all those other times. And how do we know, maybe a little less honest is good, too. I know you can do that.

MURRAY. Be less than honest?

HELEN. As if that's possible. It keeps coming out the same. You did what was good for Murray.

MURRAY. That's because Murray is such a peach of a guy someone should look out for him.

(Holds up his left arm with his right.)

Look at me and tell me I'm not useless. A comic with a stroke. This is not exactly a great career move, Helen.

HELEN. You're feeling sorry for yourself, Murray. Cut it out.
MURRAY. I'm entitled to a little self-pity. I've earned it.
HELEN. Haven't we all.
MURRAY. You didn't have a stroke.
HELEN. No, I had you.
MURRAY. I'm going back to the hospital. That male nurse with the cute behind is starting to look better and better. And he doesn't yell at me. He isn't angry at me.
HELEN. He isn't married to you.

*(**MURRAY** angrily starts wheeling himself toward the door. Because only his right arm works, he wheels in a counter-clock-wise circle. He keeps trying, however. **HELEN** sits and watches. He finally stops.)*

HELEN *(cont.)* Why'd you stop?
MURRAY. I was getting dizzy.
HELEN. Going in circles will do that.

*(**MURRAY** hangs his head and begins to cry. After some hesitation, **HELEN** goes to him and comforts him, stroking him until he stops crying.)*

MURRAY. Why are you being so nice?
HELEN. I don't know. I'm acting weirder than you. It's a sign of aging or psychosis.
MURRAY. Our life wasn't always like this.
HELEN. You're right. Sometimes we got on each other's nerves.
MURRAY. Sometimes we had good times.
HELEN. Sometimes.
MURRAY. The time I had the booking in Vegas and you went with me.
HELEN. And you lost more than you made.
MURRAY. Given what I made, that wasn't so hard to do.
HELEN. Did Jack take his percentage before or after gambling dollars?
MURRAY. Before. You should know this about show biz. It's the talent that's stupid, not the agent.

HELEN. It was fun though. Vegas in August. Everyone said they didn't mind the heat because it was dry. I never understood that. It's dry in a microwave, but that doesn't mean I want to live in one.

MURRAY. Remember, I wrote all those "it was so hot" jokes and then I played a club and the air-conditioning broke and it got down to fourteen degrees. The audience was wearing their ski jackets. They brought in meat to hang from the chandeliers.

HELEN. The slot machines paid off on three snow balls.

MURRAY. Hey, that was good, Helen. Three snow balls. I think I'll steal that one.

HELEN. Might as well. I stole it from you.

MURRAY. I don't remember that one.

HELEN. No big deal.

MURRAY. No, it is a big deal. The stroke wasn't supposed to effect my memory.

HELEN. Old age does. Don't look now, Murray, but you're getting up there.

MURRAY. That's a lie. Who told you that?

HELEN. Just a hunch.

MURRAY. Your hunch reminds me of our trip to Paris.

HELEN. Okay, I'll bite. How does my hunch remind you of our trip to Paris?

MURRAY. Your hunch back in Notre Dame.

HELEN. Awful joke, Murray, but it was a good time.

MURRAY. We did some nice traveling in those days, didn't we?

HELEN. I loved Paris.

MURRAY. Italy, Spain, England.

HELEN. Paris. Don't you remember Paris?

MURRAY. I want to remember. I just don't.

HELEN. You think I'm still upset about that little French poodle you were schmoozing with at the bar. That's why it's suddenly convenient not to remember Paris.

MURRAY. Don't remember any poodles. A cocker spaniel, once, in Madrid, maybe, but never a poodle. Their hair is too frizzy. They remind me of my old aunt Tessie. Big frizzy head of hair, like a Brillo pad on her head.

HELEN. That was a Brillo pad on her head. Not much for looks, but great for cleaning pots.

MURRAY. How come we never did a double? You've got good timing, fast thinking.

HELEN. No guts.

MURRAY. You married me.

HELEN. I didn't need guts for that. I loved you.

MURRAY. Maybe you still love me.

HELEN. Maybe you've had too much activity for one day.

MURRAY. Do you?

HELEN. What?

MURRAY. Still love me.

HELEN. You think your stroke would change how I feel about you?

MURRAY. You didn't answer.

HELEN. I thought I did.

MURRAY. Do you still love me, God damn it?

HELEN. Never more than at this touching, sensitive moment.

MURRAY. I'm doing the best I can.

HELEN. That's what worries me.

MURRAY. I'm still waiting to hear.

HELEN. I've waited 35 years. Since…

MURRAY. Yeah, I remember. Since the time you called me a sadistic…what was it?

HELEN. A sadistic son-of-a-bitch because you never, ever, told me you loved me. You married me and you never said it. And you've managed to hold out right up to now.

MURRAY. I come from a family of determined people.

HELEN. You come from a family of con artists and sadists.

MURRAY. Well, see, I never thought it was necessary. I thought it was pretty obvious how I felt about you.

HELEN. It was. Mostly.

MURRAY. Mostly? You mean the travel?

HELEN. I mean mostly and the travel is part of it. And after all these years of you holding out on me, you want to know if *I* love *you*.

MURRAY. I want to know if you *still* love me.

HELEN. What's the difference in what I said and what you said?

MURRAY. The word "still," as in "despite."

HELEN. Despite what?

MURRAY. Despite all of this. Despite the left side of my body being useless; despite having to cut my meat, feed me, take me to the toilet, dress me. Despite a sex life that is a memory.

HELEN. A pretty good memory. When you were home.

MURRAY. Despite all of that, do you still?

HELEN. Despite all of that, yes.

MURRAY. Great. Then heat up my coffee. It's too cold.

(HELEN exits to the kitchen. MURRAY waits, staring out to the audience. HELEN enters.)

HELEN. However…

MURRAY. However nothing. My coffee.

HELEN. Don't you want to hear about the "mostly."

MURRAY. First my coffee, then the "mostly."

(HELEN lifts the cup to MURRAY's lips. He drinks, and takes the cup in his good hand.)

HELEN. However…

MURRAY. Wait. Any cake left?

HELEN. Nope. *(beat)* Now?

MURRAY. You finished the last piece? I was looking forward to the cake.

HELEN. Stop with the cake. There is no more cake. Now, the mostly?

MURRAY. No cake, okay, mostly.

HELEN. While it's mostly, there are some things I don't love you for.

MURRAY. I never knew you could do that. Split up love like that. I always thought you could love or not love. All or nothing.

HELEN. Some things you like, some you don't, right? On the Oreo's you always just eat the filling and throw away the cookie.

MURRAY. Yeah, that's true.

HELEN. Why not love and not love. What, everything about you I should love? I don't love everything about me, why should I love everything about you?

MURRAY. Yeah, but over all. As a person. In total. You either love or don't.

HELEN. Nope. I always did it by piece work. Must be a carry over from my garment center days.

MURRAY. Okay, Helen, I see where this is going, so let's get to it. Let's make Dr. Shapiro really happy. What don't you love?

HELEN. Part of it I already told you.

MURRAY. My travelling.

HELEN. Yes, your travelling, but something more important, your freedom. I envied that, that you could just pick up and go, leave, not have to worry about me. Just go do your jig.

MURRAY. Gig. Gig, for crying out loud.

HELEN. Right. Do that.

MURRAY. And that's what you don't love.

HELEN. That you had no reservations about picking up and leaving me, yes that I didn't love. That your work came ahead of me, that I didn't love. Call it selfish on my part…

MURRAY. It was selfish on your part.

HELEN. …but I also knew you so well. I knew what it would lead to, the danger it put us in.

MURRAY. Danger? I was on the road telling jokes, not robbing banks.

HELEN. I think I would have preferred your robbing banks.

MURRAY. Well, that possibility is over. The get-away would be a nightmare.

HELEN. Murray, did you notice anything strange about your hospitalization?

MURRAY. I was in a coma, Helen. I figure that was pretty strange.

HELEN. You had a lot of visitors.

MURRAY. That wasn't so strange. I'm a nice guy. People like me.

HELEN. Once you were out of the coma people kept visiting, but one didn't come visit.

MURRAY. Most people in the world didn't come visit. No one from China came, not one Rockefeller showed up.

HELEN. My sister Gladys didn't come. Except for one time when you were in the coma, she never visited you.

MURRAY. Really? Okay, just for that I won't come visit her when she has her stroke. That'll show her.

HELEN. No jokes on this one Murray. How come Gladys didn't visit?

MURRAY. Seen one stroke seen 'em all?

HELEN. No jokes I said, Murray.

MURRAY. I'm trying, but I can't stop myself. This is so silly. What do you want me to say, that I'm my sister-in-law's keeper? Not only didn't I know she didn't visit, now that I know, I don't know why she didn't visit. Okay? I don't know the reason for that, I don't know the reason for my stroke, for not being able to wipe my own behind. I don't know the reason for anything, all right? And what the hell does this have to do with my freedom?

HELEN. Plenty, Murray. It's why I don't love the part of you that created this private space for yourself, this freedom to live without me. It allowed you to do stuff you couldn't if you were home.

MURRAY. I'm not getting any older, Helen. Or wiser. The point. Before I have another stroke, the point.

HELEN. Do you want to know why Gladys never came to visit?

MURRAY. Yes, yes, please, I'm begging you. Tell me. I can't stand this any more.

HELEN. Because the one time she did, I threw her ass out of the hospital.

MURRAY. What the hell did you do that for?

HELEN. Because she told me about your affair with her.

*(**MURRAY** slumps forward in his seat.)*

MURRAY!

MURRAY. *(sitting up after a pregnant pause as if nothing happened)* What?

HELEN. You scared the shit out of me.

MURRAY. I don't know what happened. I seem to remember you saying something stupid about me and Gladys. Then everything went black. With a tinge of red. Very pretty, actually.

*(**HELEN** stands over **MURRAY** and prepares to slug him. He uses his right hand to lift his left arm over his face as he cringes.)*

MURRAY *(cont.)* You going to hit a cripple? You imagine this affair with Gladys and so you'd hit a broken cripple who can't defend himself.

*(**HELEN** controls her rage, recovers and sits back down on the couch.)*

HELEN. Let me tell you my problem, Murray. I know that you and Gladys had this thing and it really frightens me that I come from the same gene pool as dopey Gladys. And, of course, it fits. It's not like you were doing anything against your nature. Snakes crawl, politicians lie, comics travel and screw around. I mean, you were just doing what all comics probably do. But not with my screwy sister.

(MURRAY vehemently shakes his head "no.")

(adamant) But here's my problem, Murray. Here I am, with you, knowing what I know, hating what you did, feeding you coffee because you don't have the strength to lift the cup. Despite the left side of your body being useless, despite having to cut your meat, feed you, take you to the toilet, dress you. Despite a sex life that is a memory. Despite all of this, here I am, your caretaker for the rest of my life. Doing all this for you for the rest of my life, knowing what I know. You put me in this position and then you ask me if I still love you. What do you think, Murray?

MURRAY. I think I never think and that's why I hurt people. I think you'll never have to worry about this again. I think you'd be right to wrap me in newspaper and throw me in the garbage. I think you'd be right to walk out.

HELEN. Good idea.

(HELEN puts on her coat.)

MURRAY. I didn't mean now.

(HELEN heads for the door.)

Where are you going?

(HELEN exits. Lights fade on MURRAY to black.)

End of Act I

ACT II

(*SETTING:* **MURRAY**'s *living room.*)

(*AT LIGHTS:* **MURRAY** *is seated in his chair. There is a knock at the door.*)

MURRAY. You walked out, now you can find your way back in.

(*Another knock.* **MURRAY** *wheels to the door.*)

You always forget something. You haven't left this place in the last five years without having to come back because you forgot something.

(**MURRAY** *opens the door and* **GLADYS** *enters.*)

GLADYS. Hi, Murray.

MURRAY. Oh, Jesus.

GLADYS. Aren't you glad to see me?

MURRAY. Have you come to finish me off?

GLADYS. I didn't realize the stroke caused you to be so suspicious.

MURRAY. It has nothing to do with the stroke. I know danger when I see it. You've done some job on me, Gladys.

GLADYS. She told you?

MURRAY. In spades. We just had this big blow out and then she left. You just missed her.

GLADYS. I know. I waited outside until she left.

MURRAY. You couldn't miss her. She had steam coming out of her ears.

GLADYS. It'll blow over, Murray.

MURRAY. I guess she'll be back. She didn't pack a bag. I think she went out to buy a gun.

GLADYS. I've been hanging around for weeks for this opportunity. She never leaves you alone.

MURRAY. She said she knows now what happens when she does. And look. She right. She leaves and you show up. She's brilliant, don't you think?

GLADYS. That's what I've always said.

MURRAY. You better leave. If she comes back and finds us we'll be on the front page of tomorrow's Post.

GLADYS. I came to see how you were doing.

MURRAY. My doctor thinks I'm going to live. He doesn't know Helen.

GLADYS. Don't be upset.

MURRAY. Upset? Why would I be upset? What makes you think I'm upset?

GLADYS. Good, because…

MURRAY. I need a gun, because I can't strangle you with one hand.

GLADYS. In the long run you'll see what I did is for the best.

MURRAY. What long run? Take a good look. I don't have a long run. The long run is behind me. I'm in the short run now, Gladys. And you've just made it shorter. When did this happen?

GLADYS. Ah, you've forgotten. It began in Jersey, Murray.

MURRAY. No, you dope. When did you tell Helen?

GLADYS. I don't like the tone of your voice.

MURRAY. Tone? What tone? This is rage, Gladys. When did you tell her?

GLADYS. While you were in the hospital.

MURRAY. Given your great need for tact and honesty I'll bet it was when I was in a coma.

GLADYS. I thought that was the best time.

MURRAY. Why? You figured I was going to die?

GLADYS. You always knew me like an open book.

MURRAY. That suddenly is written in Greek.

GLADYS. I don't understand what you are so angry about. Shouldn't adults behave like adults?

MURRAY. Yes, if they're sane. Now I understand what Helen has been so upset about.

GLADYS. I know she didn't take it well, but at least *she* didn't threaten to kill me.

MURRAY. Not you, Gladys. She wants to kill me.

GLADYS. Don't be silly.

MURRAY. Don't be naive.

GLADYS. Despite all of this, you seem to be doing okay.

MURRAY. Dr. Shapiro, that putz, thinks I'm depressed. Helen believes him.

GLADYS. You have every right to be depressed. Look what you've gone through.

MURRAY. Somehow, at this point in our lives, I don't think she cares to understand that.

GLADYS. Helen was there for you every single day, Murray.

MURRAY. I know, but somehow lately she seems a little bitter.

GLADYS. She's been through a lot, too.

MURRAY. You were always so understanding. One of your virtues.

GLADYS. I try. How do I look?

MURRAY. Don't change the subject.

GLADYS. How do I look?

MURRAY. You know you always were good to look at, Gladys. I guess you still are.

GLADYS. Guess?

MURRAY. Okay, you are.

GLADYS. What?

MURRAY. You are still good to look at. Now, let's get back to…

GLADYS. We did have fun, didn't we, Murray?

MURRAY. Right now my life is going down the toilet and you want to talk about the good old days.

GLADYS. Remember the weekend you played at the Jersey shore and I drove down to meet you?

MURRAY. That was some weekend.

GLADYS. The walks on the beach.

MURRAY. Think you could push this damn thing through the sand, Gladys?

GLADYS. Let's just remember the good times, Murray. Like being together after the show.

MURRAY. Great sex, then sleeping late, breakfast in bed.

GLADYS. You always told me I was the best.

MURRAY. I never realized you'd be the last. I also never realized you'd be the cause of my death.

GLADYS. You never would tell me if there were others before me.

MURRAY. A comic never admits to anything.

GLADYS. Time to make a clean slate, Murray.

MURRAY. Look what your cleaning the slate accomplished.

GLADYS. I did what I thought best. I have a clear conscience.

MURRAY. It's nice to know one of us is so fucking happy.

GLADYS. And now it's your turn, Murray. So…were there others?

MURRAY. A couple. They meant nothing. The road is lonely.

GLADYS. There's nothing to be ashamed of, Murray.

MURRAY. That's right. You try spending a week-end in Dubuque. See the rusty cannon by city hall and visit the Wal-Mart and that's about it.

GLADYS. So you needed companionship.

MURRAY. That's right. And…I also wanted to get laid.

GLADYS. All perfectly understandable.

MURRAY. But I didn't lie, Gladys. You were the best.

GLADYS. Thank you, Murray. Now, don't you feel better having told me? Doesn't clearing the air make you feel cleaner?

MURRAY. Maybe it's me, but I still don't feel like dancing.

GLADYS. You will, Murray. Sometimes these things take time. It's only been a couple of weeks since you got out of the hospital.

MURRAY. Somehow today seems like a couple of weeks.

GLADYS. I think I better leave. Helen might be coming home soon.

MURRAY. Might be a good idea.

GLADYS. Are you sorry I came?

MURRAY. I'm glad you came. I'm glad to know what's going on. I'm glad to know that my one time lover has the brains of a flea; that she broke the cardinal rule of affairs: never admit it. If Helen had walked in on us in bed, I would have denied it. If she had to pull us apart, I would have denied it. But you, you decide honesty is the best policy, that it's okay to break the cardinal rule, a rule that was handed down from the time of the cavemen and has been honored as one of the cornerstones of marriage: never admit.

GLADYS. Are you finished?

MURRAY. You have a rebuttal?

GLADYS. You are both acting like children. *(rises to leave)* Give my regards to Helen. Tell her I have no hard feelings and I'll be in touch.

MURRAY. Wait. Sit down. I don't know what to tell her. Stay and help me.

GLADYS. I can't stay in a place where I'm yelled at, threatened, made fun of. I have issues with self respect as it is and I don't need any more attacks. For some reason you both think I have purposely set out to destroy your marriage when all I wanted to do was do the honorable thing.

*(**GLADYS** heads for the door.)*

MURRAY. You're not going to stay and help me?

GLADYS. Murray, you took me to bed. I didn't take you. You're the one who cheated on his wife, not me. You figure it out. I'm leaving.

*(**GLADYS** exits.)*

*(Lights dim, then relight. **MURRAY** is gone, **HELEN** is pacing. A loud knocking at the door. **HELEN** rushes for the door.)*

HELEN. Okay, okay. Coming.

*(**HELEN** opens the door to let in a frazzled **GLADYS**.)*

GLADYS. What do you mean he's missing?

HELEN. What part of that word don't you understand? Missing. As in "gone." He was here, now he's not. Missing.

GLADYS. How does a man with a stroke in a wheelchair become missing from his own home?

HELEN. I went food shopping for fruit. Gone tops two hours…

GLADYS. Two hours shopping for fruit?

HELEN. Yeah, why?

GLADYS. Were you waiting for the fruit to ripen?

HELEN. Jokes? I get jokes?

GLADYS. It is a long time.

HELEN. Okay, I also sat on a bench and thought.

GLADYS. About what?

HELEN. About Einstein's concept of the time-space continuum. What's your opinion?

GLADYS. You're being nasty.

HELEN. And you ask the dumbest questions of any human over the age of six. I was thinking about Murray, me, you. Triangles. Under what circumstances is murder justified? How will I look in prison grey? How did I get into this situation? You know, the usual stuff people my age think about after buying fruit.

GLADYS. Okay, then what?

HELEN. I come home and he's not here.

GLADYS. Where did he go?

HELEN. Where did he…You're useless. Get out.

GLADYS. I will not.

HELEN. Then stop asking stupid questions. If I knew where he was, he wouldn't be missing. That's what missing means. You are a college graduate, Gladys. Try and think back to one of your classes where they might have discussed the concept "missing" as in your intelligence.

GLADYS. You called me, you must have wanted me, so stop insulting me.

HELEN. I'm still angry.

GLADYS. I understand, just stop...

HELEN. Okay, okay. I'm sorry. You're just such an easy target.

GLADYS. Do you want me to go home?

HELEN. *(angry)* No.

GLADYS. *(angry)* Okay, then I'll stay.

HELEN. *(angry)* Good.

GLADYS. Did you call Brenda?

HELEN. Not yet. I didn't want to alarm her.

GLADYS. So you called to alarm me.

HELEN. The truth? I thought maybe he was with you.

GLADYS. Why would you think that?

HELEN. BECAUSE YOU WERE FUCKING HIM FOR CHRIST'S SAKE.

*(**GLADYS** starts to leave.)*

Stop. I just thought that since you and he...

GLADYS. Well, we're not, okay? What kind of a person do you take me for?

(The stare at each other for a while.)

HELEN. Do you want to reconsider that question?

GLADYS. Never mind, Helen. I understand. Let's change the subject, shall we?

HELEN. Yes, let's change the subject.

GLADYS. Good. When did this happen?

HELEN. Five, six o'clock. Something like that. I come home, gone.

GLADYS. Then he was alone for about an hour.

HELEN. Two hours.

GLADYS. One hour.

HELEN. What are you talking about? I said I was gone for two hours. That means Murray was alone for two hours. Get it?

GLADYS. I was here.

HELEN. Where?

GLADYS. Here.

HELEN. In my house?

GLADYS. For a while.

HELEN. With my husband?

GLADYS. We just talked.

HELEN. After all of this, you have the nerve to come here to be with him when I'm not here.

GLADYS. I waited for you to leave. I didn't want to start any fights with you in front of Murray.

HELEN. What a relief.

GLADYS. Don't be sarcastic.

HELEN. I still don't understand why you came here?

GLADYS. I told you. To talk.

HELEN. That's why someone invented the telephone. People can use phones to talk to other people. When *you* visit someone, you seem to have other things in mind.

GLADYS. I also wanted to see how he was getting along.

HELEN. He's getting along just fine, thank you.

GLADYS. He seemed depressed.

HELEN. Your powers of observation continually astound me.

GLADYS. Stop the sarcasm or I'm leaving.

HELEN. What did you talk about?

GLADYS. Things.

HELEN. Let me re-phrase that. What did you talk about?

GLADYS. I told him.

HELEN. You told him what?

GLADYS. I told him. You know.

HELEN. I do? How? I wasn't here, remember? You were here alone with my husband, one of your many conquests, but one of the few without an M.D. after their names. How would I know what you told him?

GLADYS. Because I told him what I told you that day in the hospital.

HELEN. My God, what did he say?

GLADYS. He insulted me.

HELEN. Is that possible?

GLADYS. Believe it or not, I am a sensitive person.

HELEN. Okay, I don't believe it.

GLADYS. Doesn't matter. Since I know what I'm doing is right, I don't let it effect me.

HELEN. Water off a duck's back.

GLADYS. That's right.

HELEN. You were always such a self-righteous *prima dona*.

GLADYS. Your attacking me will not speed up our finding Murray.

HELEN. It doesn't have to be one or the other, Gladys.

GLADYS. Have it your own way.

HELEN. If I do, it will be for the first time.

GLADYS. Did Murray have any money?

(**HELEN** *checks a drawer in a piece of the living room furniture.*)

HELEN. There was about twenty dollars in there. It's gone.

GLADYS. He's not going to get far on twenty dollars.

HELEN. Maybe he's not looking to get far.

GLADYS. What does that mean?

HELEN. He must have told you we had a fight this morning. About you. I walked out. Even you were able to see how depressed he is. Maybe he's going to do something to himself.

GLADYS. He got depressed about me?

HELEN. Don't flatter yourself. He got depressed about himself. No, he got *more* depressed about himself.

GLADYS. Well, if it will make you feel better, I always felt that beneath all the jokes he was also depressed when he was with me.

HELEN. Gee, that makes me feel a whole lot better, Gladys. *(pause to reflect)* You think I should call the police?

GLADYS. Brenda first. Then the police.

(**HELEN** *heads for the phone, stops.*)

HELEN. He's not at Brenda's.

GLADYS. How do you know? Call her.

HELEN. She went to Kansas City with her boy-friend.

GLADYS. What's in Kansas City?

HELEN. The Yankees. They went to watch the Yankees play baseball in Kansas City.

GLADYS. Wouldn't it have easier to go to Yankee stadium. It's only a half hour away.

HELEN. They also wanted to eat ribs.

GLADYS. They went to Kansas City to eat ribs? The ribs in Memphis are much better. Drier, you know.

HELEN. Myself, I always like the ribs…Do you hear this? Are you listening to this? We really are sisters, Gladys. Murray is missing, wandering around New York, able to use only one arm, in a wheel chair, with twenty dollars, depressed like the Grand Canyon, and we're talking about ribs. This is scary nuts.

(**HELEN** *goes to the phone.*)

GLADYS. Who you calling?

HELEN. His doctor. Maybe he went there.

GLADYS. He called Shapiro a putz, so he probably didn't go there.

HELEN. You were only here for an hour, but you guys really covered the bases. Is there anything you don't know?

GLADYS. Some things.

HELEN. Like what?

GLADYS. Personal things.

HELEN. Hey, we're sisters aren't we? Or are we? I'm not sure anymore.

GLADYS. I don't know how to stay married, for one.

HELEN. You don't have to. You have other women's husbands to keep you occupied.

GLADYS. You've been married to Murray for over thirty-five years. I never made it past ten. With three of them. And now Murray.

HELEN. Am I supposed to feel sorry for you, Gladys?

GLADYS. Would that be so terrible?

HELEN. At the moment, yes. Try me in a month. Better make that a year.

GLADYS. I guess I'm also telling you I admire you.

HELEN. Which makes what you did all the crazier. Him I understand. Right now I hate him for putting me through this, but for you to do this to me…I don't understand it.

GLADYS. I think it's because in some ways I'm like a man.

HELEN. Not that I noticed.

GLADYS. Thank you.

HELEN. I didn't mean that to be a compliment.

GLADYS. Davey…remember Davey?

HELEN. Your first.

GLADYS. Right. He said men have a special problem most women don't have.

HELEN. They have to stand up to pee?

GLADYS. Close. He said they can either think with their brains or think with…you know…their other thing. But they can't do both at the same time.

HELEN. It's one or the other?

GLADYS. Exactly.

HELEN. And that's supposed to be you?

GLADYS. Not supposed to be, Helen. That is me. Over and over and over. When I was with Murray I stopped thinking. He wasn't your husband. He was a man and he was a great…

HELEN. Don't finish that sentence, Gladys. Don't even think of finishing that sentence.

GLADYS. I think Murray has the same problem.

HELEN. So you are using stupidity as a defense? A brain disengaged from it's body?

GLADYS. That's it.

HELEN. So then which part of you should I destroy? The part that doesn't think or the part that does the work? Because some part of you has to be accountable for this.

GLADYS. Are you so innocent in all of this?

HELEN. You're saying I brought you two together? That this is my fault?

GLADYS. I'm saying a man doesn't stray unless he has a reason.

HELEN. Ah, the TV pop-psychologist speaks. Tell me, oh wise psychology guru, what did I do wrong?

GLADYS. I don't know. I wasn't in your bedroom. Apparently neither was Murray.

HELEN. Of course not. He was in yours.

GLADYS. You don't suppose he's with another woman now, do you?

HELEN. Of course, Gladys. You just solved the case. Murray's probably just went out to knock off a piece. A sixty year old guy with a stroke in a wheel-chair going out to pick up babes. Brilliant.

(There's a knock at the door. **HELEN** *opens it and* **MURRAY** *wheels himself in. He looks even more depressed, if possible.)*

Where the hell have you been?

MURRAY. I wouldn't have come home, but I had *(realizes* **GLADYS** *is there and gets hesitant)* no place else...to...go.

*(***MURRAY** *looks at* **GLADYS**. *The he looks at* **HELEN**. *Then back to* **GLADYS**. *Then he heads back to the door.* **HELEN** *blocks his way.)*

HELEN. No you don't, you selfish, self-centered, narcissistic, ego-maniacal...

GLADYS. I think all those mean essentially the same thing, Helen.

*(***MURRAY** *nods his head in eager agreement.)*

HELEN. How dare you leave here without telling me where you're going?

MURRAY. Why? I need your permission?

HELEN. You didn't hear a word I said to you this morning, did you?

MURRAY. Yeah, sure I did. You asked me if I wanted a piece of cake. I never got it so I decided to...

HELEN. I don't want to hear it you lying, manipulative...

MURRAY. *(to* **GLADYS***)* See, did I tell you. She treats me like shit. What are you doing here?

GLADYS. Helen called me. She thought you were with me.

MURRAY. Why would I be with you?

GLADYS. That's what I told her. But she…

(**HELEN** *sits and begins to sob. After a few beats,* **GLADYS** *walks to her and comforts her.*)

MURRAY. I went to Starbucks.

HELEN. *(stunned)* What?

MURRAY. Starbucks. I went to get some coffee and *(to* **HELEN***)* CAKE.

GLADYS. For cake? Starbucks has lousy cake. World Coffee is much better. Also the coffee at Starbucks gives me gas.

MURRAY. *(to* **HELEN** *in disbelief)* You two are really sisters?

HELEN. I'm going to have a DNA study made.

MURRAY. She's right about the cake, though. Stale.

HELEN. You were gone two hours.

GLADYS. *You* were gone two hours. He was only gone one hour.

HELEN. Of course, I forgot. Thank you, Gladys. Still, that's a lot of cake, Murray.

MURRAY. I needed to get out to think.

GLADYS. It took you a whole hour to think. It never takes me that long to think.

MURRAY. Somehow I think I knew that, Gladys.

HELEN. Gladys, I thank you for coming over and spending quality time with me, but I think Murray and I have some things to talk over. So, if you don't mind…

MURRAY. Not yet, Helen. I want you both here for a while. Please sit down.

(**HELEN** *and* **GLADYS** *sit.*)

I went because I also needed to get back to my work.

HELEN. Work? You haven't had a jig in…

MURRAY. Gig. True, but I needed to *try* and get back to my work. I needed to start writing again. Not much, just a beginning. So I went to have some coffee and *(to* **HELEN***)* CAKE and to start writing.

GLADYS. Oh, Murray, that's great. I'm so happy for you. You're writing jokes again.

MURRAY. At first it was more like observations about my life.

HELEN. About our great lives together, our fabulous marriage, how terrific it is to have a loving sister? Observations? As I recall, most of your observations begin and end with tits and ass.

MURRAY. For some reason that doesn't seem to be such an important thing now.

GLADYS. It's true. As we get older our priorities change. I know that I look at life...

HELEN. Gladys, sister dear, ordinarily I would be fascinated by your comments about life, but now let's let Murray finish. I think he's trying to tell us something profound. Aren't you Murray?

GLADYS. Well, I don't think your tone is going to help any, Helen.

MURRAY. No, no, Gladys, Helen is right. She should be pissed off and I am trying to say something. How profound, I don't know.

HELEN. Go ahead, Murray. You've got all the rope you need.

MURRAY. *(after a pause to collect his thoughts)* Gladys, when we were seeing each other did it ever seem to you that Helen was in the room? Right there. Right with us.

GLADYS. Helen would never do anything so kinky.

MURRAY. Not for real. More like a spirit.

GLADYS. Never crossed my mind. *(to* **HELEN***)* Oh, no offense, Helen, but when I'm with someone, I'm only with that one. As I said before, at such times I tend not to think with my brain, but with my...you know. *(to* **MURRAY***)* Why would I think about Helen when I'm with you, Murray?

MURRAY. Good question, Gladys. I'm not sure, except I always felt her presence in that room. Is that weird, or what? Sitting in a chair right there with us. The whole time.

HELEN. Doing what? Nodding approvingly? Applauding? Videotaping?

MURRAY. No. Just sitting. I couldn't shake the feeling.

GLADYS. Sounds creepy to me.

HELEN. Be quiet, Gladys. Okay, I was sitting there. Let's move on.

MURRAY. Now I have to wonder, if I felt Helen sitting there, what was I doing?

HELEN. *(calmly, matter-of-fact)* You were screwing Gladys, Murray. I thought we all understood that.

GLADYS. That's disgusting, Helen.

HELEN. Then why'd you do it, Gladys?

MURRAY. Can I continue? *(He pauses as **HELEN** and **GLADYS** compose themselves.)* Now I figure that since I had an audience, I must have been performing.

GLADYS. And doing a really nice…

HELEN. *(menacing to **GLADYS**)* I'm warning you, Gladys.

MURRAY. Can I please continue?

HELEN. *(with a nasty look at **GLADYS**)* Of course, dear.

MURRAY. Where was I?

HELEN. You were performing. *(beat)* In bed. *(beat)* With a side-kick. *(beat)* Just like Abbott and Costello. Or even better, like Laurel and Hardy. And I always thought you did a single.

MURRAY. That's exactly right, Helen. No offence, Gladys, but even with you, it was a single.

GLADYS. You're a liar. No one could fake it like that.

MURRAY. Oh, don't get me wrong. I enjoyed it. It's just that with you I never felt something I felt with Helen. With Helen I felt connected. With Helen it wasn't a single. With you I felt I was on stage, performing.

HELEN. Well, Murray, thanks for the complement, but if you think I'm going to ask what kind of review you got, think again, sport.

MURRAY. It doesn't matter. What matters is that with you I never felt I was performing.

GLADYS. I think I'm insulted. *(to **HELEN**)* Should I be insulted?

MURRAY. So that's what I was writing in Starbucks. I was writing about the difference I felt, trying to understand it.

HELEN. And?

MURRAY. Once I realized that there was a difference between you and Gladys, about how I felt different with each of you, something changed in me. I felt I could write material again. I felt I could be creative again.

*(**MURRAY** takes a piece of paper out of his shirt pocket.)*

Picture this. A comedy club. "And now, a man known for his fast wit and faster wheels, Mr. Murray Green." And I wheel myself out to the center of the stage. The audience is stunned. A guy with a stroke in a wheel chair. What the hell could this guy say that's funny. A disaster waiting to happen. The audience is groaning, looking for a way out, ordering more drinks to block me out. I threaten their good time. My mic is down front and is three feet over my head. I start to talk and the crowd can't hear me. I show I realize this and start to look worried. The crowd starts to feel sorry for me. I grab the mic and lower it into my lap. I keep my head lowered, staring at the mic. The audience thinks I'm crying. Then I slowly look up, leer at them and I say, "Anyone want to give a cripple a blow job." They will go nuts.

*(**HELEN** starts to speak, but is cut off by **MURRAY**.)*

MURRAY *(cont.)* Wait, Helen. I've just gotten started. So then, then, I begin with the usual crap jokes, but everyone knows it's crap, see. Like, "a funny thing happened on my way to the club tonight. I had a stroke." Rim shot. Then, "I just flew in from the coast and is my arm tired." Rim shot. Then, maybe I use, "A bum came up to me tonight and gave *me* a quarter.'" Get it. I turn all the old crap into a parody of my old act. If these jokes ever had hair, by now they're bald. Then maybe a song, some old standard, like "Somebody loves me, I wonder why." Or, maybe the Beatles song, "I Want to Use Your Hand." Or that other Beatles tune, "No Where Man."

HELEN. Stop it, Murray.

MURRAY. No, wait.

HELEN. I don't like this.

MURRAY. Just listen. See, I'm sitting in this Starbucks, working on this new routine, but I'm also watching all the young ass go by and I'm getting an erection.

(**HELEN** *and* **GLADYS** *react to this with disbelief.*)

I swear. It was amazing. Well, not so amazing. In fact, it wasn't much of an erection, but it was a beginning.

GLADYS. Well, considering what you've gone through, I think that's quite an accomplishment.

HELEN. I'll call Mike Wallace.

MURRAY. Anyway I'm sitting there as stunned as you two are about what's happening, when it suddenly occurs to me that even though I got this thing going on in my head and my pants, these young girls didn't give a shit if I lived or died. To them I'm just an old piece of meat waiting to die.

HELEN. Okay, I'm not liking what I hear, Murray.

MURRAY. Then I think, so what am I doing here. I should be going home. But then I suddenly remembered something else and this sealed it. Helen, you were right this morning.

HELEN. About?

MURRAY. You said I never told you I loved you. And you were right. All these years, I never told you I loved you.

GLADYS. If it will make you feel better, Helen, he never told me either.

HELEN. Gladys, will you shut up?

MURRAY. Remember what you told me this morning, Helen? Knowing what you know now, hating what I did, feeding me coffee because I couldn't hold the cup, having to cut my meat, feed me, take me to the toilet, dress me, a sex life that's a memory, despite all of that having to be my caretaker. That's what you said, Helen. And then I had the balls to ask you if you loved *me*.

HELEN. I just figured it was in character.

MURRAY. Exactly so, Helen. So what I came to realize in that Starbucks was that in addition to everything else that's wrong with me, I'm also a stupid, old man. Do you remember one of my early shticks, the one about thinking my name was "stupid."

HELEN. I remember. You used it in the Catskills.

GLADYS. And in Jersey.

HELEN. An oldie, but goodie.

MURRAY. I need to finish, ladies, so if you please. Yes, Helen. I love you. I've always loved you. Despite Gladys, sorry Gladys, despite Gladys and despite my selfishness I always loved you and I always will. That's what I discovered. And I'm not saying that because I need you. I'm saying that because I want you.

(There is a significant pause as **HELEN** *thinks this over.)*

HELEN. Gladys, could you make us some coffee.

GLADYS. First, I'd like to say that…

HELEN. You know where everything is. Murray would like some cake, too.

GLADYS. Well, I'd just like to say…

HELEN. Now, Gladys.

*(***GLADYS** *exits to the kitchen.)*

Do you expect me to buy all of that?

MURRAY. I don't know what to expect.

HELEN. After all that happened this morning, you meet Gladys in our home…

MURRAY. I didn't invite her.

HELEN. You didn't throw her out.

MURRAY. No. I wanted her to stay to help me deal with you.

HELEN. You're afraid of me?

MURRAY. No. I'm afraid of hurting you again. I'm afraid of losing you.

HELEN. Because of your stroke.

MURRAY. Because I love you. You don't have to believe that, but after thirty years of marriage...

HELEN. Thirty-five, but who's counting?

MURRAY. ...and never saying it, to have me say that twice to you in less than five minutes must count for something.

HELEN. Yes, but I'm not sure what. You'll understand if I'm a little leery of jumping to conclusions.

GLADYS *(O.S.)* I can't find the cake.

HELEN. It's in the freezer.

MURRAY. You told me we didn't have any cake.

HELEN. I lied.

MURRAY. Why didn't you want to hear my material. It's good stuff.

GLADYS *(O.S.)* Where in the freezer?

HELEN. Behind the chickens. *(to* **MURRAY***)* Because I didn't want you to be hurt.

MURRAY. Why would I be hurt?

HELEN. Because whoever heard of a comic in a wheel-chair? They'll laugh at you.

MURRAY. Exactly. Besides, have you seen the crap that passes for comedy today? Helen, even in a wheel-chair I can kick these kids' asses. I'm calling Jack in the morning.

GLADYS *(O.S.)* Why do you have so many chickens?

HELEN. JUST GET THE GOD DAMN CAKE, GLADYS. *(to* **MURRAY***)* You think Jack can get you work?

MURRAY. I may not be able to travel, but there are plenty of clubs in the area. You'll drive me. I'll even invite Shapiro.

GLADYS *(O.S.)* Got it.

HELEN. The girl is a whip.

MURRAY. Just like her sister. The first time we met I told you you were smart.

HELEN. I don't remember that. I certainly don't feel that way now.

MURRAY. I also asked you if smart people ever have doubts or do they know everything?

HELEN. Now I remember. I said smart people have doubts.

MURRAY. And I asked if you ever have doubts?

HELEN. I said is this one of those Aristotle was a man, Aristotle was a Greek routines?

MURRAY. Well, do you ever have doubts?

HELEN. Of course I do. Certainly about you.

MURRAY. That's what I was afraid of.

GLADYS *(O.S.)* Almost ready.

HELEN. But smart people learn to live with doubt. It's also exciting.

(beat)

How about a walk, Murray? It's still a beautiful day. The sun is still out. A bit of a nip in the air, but nothing we can't handle.

MURRAY. That might be nice.

HELEN. Maybe we'll go to that coffee place. I've never been there. How's the coffee?

MURRAY. Tastes like battery acid, but then again it's better than yours.

HELEN. How's the cake?

MURRAY. Stale, but better than nothing.

HELEN. Better put on this scarf, Murray. There might be a breeze.

(They head for the door.)

MURRAY. You'll watch out for that dog. He pees on me again, I'll kill him.

HELEN. I'll do it for you, Murray.

*(They exit. **GLADYS** enters, carrying some cups and plates, looks around. Lights fade to black.)*

The End

PROPERTY

Typical middle-class living room furnishings
Wheel-chair
Hospital wrist I.D. bracelet
Scissors
Tray
2 cups/saucers
Slice of cake/cake plate/fork
Wrist watch for **MURRAY**

COSTUMES

MURRAY: Clothing appropriate for the Fall: Jacket, hat, scarf.
HELEN: As above.
GLADYS: As above, but gaudier, younger, with more jewelry than Helen.

**Also by
Henry Meyerson...**

Beware the Man Eating Chicken

**Fresh Brewed:
Tales from the Coffee Bar**

Proceed To Checkout

Please visit our website **samuelfrench.com** for complete descriptions and licensing information

OTHER TITLES AVAILABLE FROM SAMUEL FRENCH

JACK GOES BOATING
Bob Glaudini

Full Length / Comedy / 2m, 2f / Interior

Four flawed but likeable lower-middle-class New Yorkers interact in a touching and warmhearted play about learning how to stay afloat in the deep water of day-to-day living. Laced with cooking classes, swimming lessons and a smorgasbord of illegal drugs, *Jack Goes Boating* is a story of date panic, marital meltdown, betrayal, and the prevailing grace of the human spirit.

"An immensely likable play [that] exudes a wry compassion."
- *The New York Times*

"Endearing romantic comedy about a married couple and the social-misfit friends they fix up. Witty and knowing and all heart."
- *Variety*

"Glides effortlessly from the shallow end of the emotional pool to the deep end."
- *Theatremania.com*

SAMUELFRENCH.COM

www.ingramcontent.com/pod-product-compliance
Lightning Source LLC
Chambersburg PA
CBHW070650300426
44111CB00013B/2360